Fire Trucks

BY CYNTHIA AMOROSO

The Child's World®

Published by The Child's World®
1980 Lookout Drive • Mankato, MN 56003-1705
800-599-READ • www.childsworld.com

Acknowledgments
The Child's World®: Mary Berendes, Publishing Director
The Design Lab: Design
Jody Jensen Shaffer; Editing

Photos
Flashon Studio/Shutterstock.com: 8; James Group
Studios/iStock.com: 11; John Cairns/iStock.com: 15;
Keith Muratori/Shutterstock.com: 16; kingjon/iStock.
com: 20; Le Do/Shutterstock.com: cover, 1; Leonardo
Patrizi/iStock.com: 12; Pier Giorgio Mariani/
iStock.com: 4; shorrocks/iStock.com: 19; Talton
Photography/iStock.com: 7

ISBN 9781623239688
LCCN 2013947254

Printed in the United States of America
Mankato, MN
July, 2014
PA02237

Contents

This fire truck is on its way to an emergency in New York.

What are fire trucks?

Fire trucks are special kinds of trucks. They are used for putting out fires. They are used for other kinds of **emergencies**, too.

What do fire trucks look like?

Fire trucks are big. Most fire trucks are painted bright colors. Many of them are bright red. Some are yellow. Bright colors make the trucks easy to see.

Firefighters keep the trucks clean. They wash and shine them.

FIRE - RESCUE

53

Firefighters must wear lots of protective gear, no matter what the emergency is.

Where does the driver ride?

The driver sits in the **cab** of the truck. The cab has lots of **controls** for running the truck. It has places for other firefighters to sit, too.

How does a fire truck move?

Fire trucks move like other trucks. An **engine** gives them power. The engine burns **diesel fuel**. The engine's power moves the truck's big wheels. The driver uses a steering wheel to turn the truck.

Most fire engines can go up to 70 miles per hour (about 113 kph).

A fire truck's lights and loud sirens let people know to get out of the way.

Fire trucks must get to emergencies quickly. They need to let other drivers know they are coming—fast! They have bright flashing lights. They also have loud **sirens** and horns.

Are there different kinds of fire trucks?

There are many kinds of fire trucks. They do different kinds of jobs. Pumpers spray lots of water. Some pumpers carry big tanks full of water. They also carry hoses and tools for fighting fires. They carry masks and air for the firefighters to breathe.

This firefighter is watching over a truck's many hoses.

Ladder trucks like this one can take firefighters over 300 feet (91 m) high!

Other fire trucks are made for reaching high places. Their long ladders can reach high windows and rooftops. Some have **platforms** where firefighters can stand. These trucks carry firefighting tools, too.

Rescue trucks help save people's lives. They rescue people from fires, floods, car crashes, and other dangers. They carry tools for freeing people who are trapped. They carry supplies for helping people who are hurt.

Rescue trucks have the Jaws of Life. These tools help free people who are trapped.

FIRE · RESCUE

Emergency Medical Unit

AID

Fire trucks make our neighborhoods safer.

Are fire trucks important?

Fire trucks are very important Firefighters face many dangers. Fire trucks help them do their jobs better and more safely. Fire trucks save lives every day!

GLOSSARY

cab (KAB) A machine's cab is the area where the driver sits.

controls (kun-TROHLZ) Controls are parts that people use to run a machine.

diesel fuel (DEE-sul FYOOL) Diesel fuel is a heavy oil that is burned to make power.

emergencies (eh-MUR-jen-seez) Emergencies are times of danger, when people must act quickly.

engine (EN-jun) An engine is a machine that makes something move.

platforms (PLAT-formz) Platforms are raised, flat areas.

rescue (RES-kyoo) To rescue people is to save them from danger.

sirens (SY-renz) Sirens make loud noises to let people know there is danger.

BOOKS

Bingham, Caroline. *Fire Truck*. New York: DK Publishing, 2003.

Boucher, Jerry. *Fire Truck Nuts and Bolts*. Minneapolis, MN: Carolrhoda Books, 1993.

Coppendale, Jean. *Fire Trucks and Rescue Vehicles*. Richmond Hill, ON: Firefly Books, 2010.

Slater, Teddy. *All Aboard Fire Trucks*. New York: Platt & Munk, 1991.

WEB SITES

Visit our Web site for lots of links about fire trucks:
childsworld.com/links

Note to parents, teachers, and librarians: We routinely check our Web links to make sure they're safe, active sites—so encourage your readers to check them out!

INDEX

ABOUT THE AUTHOR

Even as a child, Cynthia Amoroso knew she wanted to be a writer. She is always working to involve kids in reading and writing, and she loves spending time in the children's section of the library or bookstore. Cynthia enjoys gardening, traveling, and having fun with friends and family.